TORN PAGES

Published by BooxAi
ISBN: 978-965-578-353-7

TORN PAGES

EUGENE MINNIFIELD JR.

Torn Pages

Written By: Eugene Minnifield Jr.

Torn Pages

Written By: Eugene Minnifield Jr.

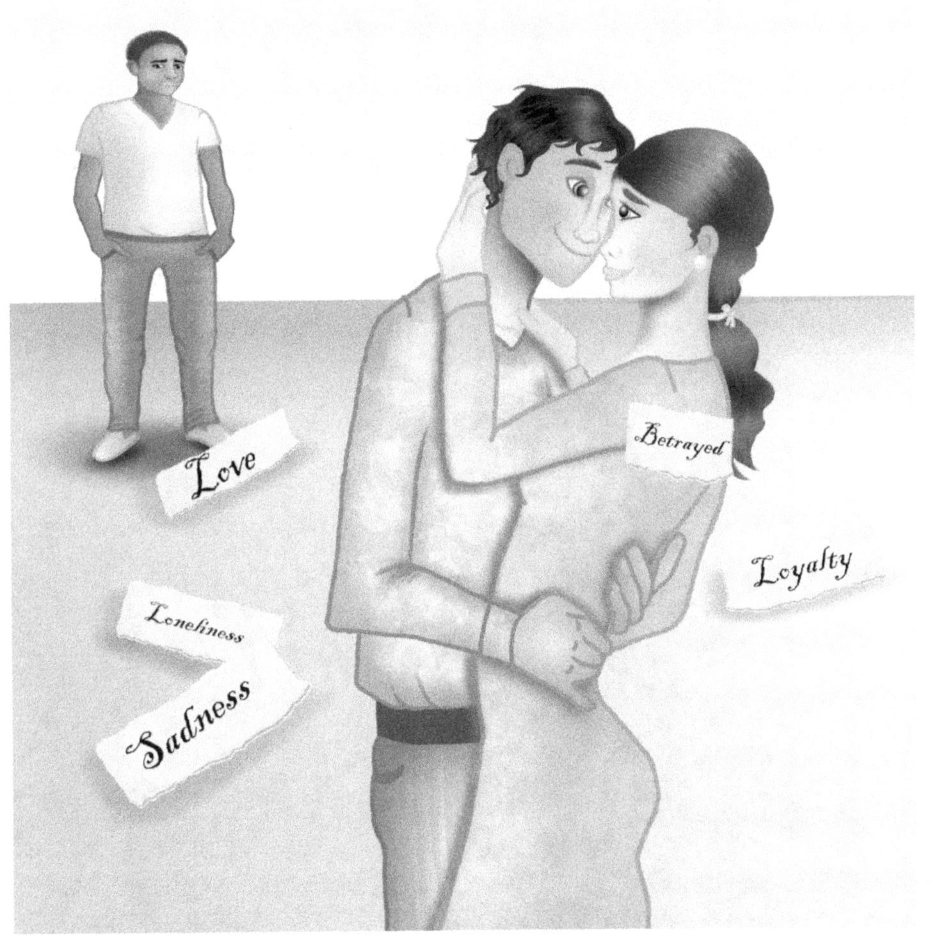

DEDICATION

This book is dedicated to my new-found love...
You!!!!

Torn Pages is about walking away and starting over while embracing who you are. Many have lost touch with what's important. The Process of love is never easy after two people have given of themselves. What will it take just to let someone else in? I hope these Poems will allow you to move past your pain.

THE PROCESS

Your response showed me how much you cared.

<u>This LOVE</u>

Words could never describe this feeling,
There were days it was hard to function,
My thoughts were in the clouds,
She accepted who I was,
And understood my past.
Her LOVE made me a better man,
Our conversations allowed me to understand,
Why I fell in LOVE so fast,
It was more than just a feeling,
A lifetime of getting answers from past
situations,
I was able to accept or feel like,
My past was a complete failure,
Or was it me learning how to lLOVE myself?

When I needed you, When love felt so real, when i wanted
to give you the world, you walked away

Until the End

The crazy thing about love is it changes you. It will make those who say they love you really think about loving you. Everyone is not built to work through the ups and downs. They cannot stand the rain or fight till the end, so don't get upset when they walk away; it's just a sign that they never understood how to *LOVE*.

Diamond in the Rough

Trying to make someone love should never be an option,
Everyone was built to love and be loved, If they don't see your
worth now, don't wait around trying to prove who you are.

I`m exhausted trying to prove my love- - one day, you will look
back and realize who I was.

One Day at a Time

Taking the time to deal with your feelings is never easy,
Time has been invested along with broken promises,
But it's not the end of the world as we embrace this moment,
Reading text messages that left your heart skipping a beat,
Now sends you crying between the sheets,
Trying to put the broken pieces together: *What happened? How did
we get here?*
One day, after moving past this pain, it will all make sense.
These tears have become my best friend as I watched you
walk away

Unconditional Love

Loving someone *never* made them stick around or do what's
right,
If they cannot get something out of loving you or want to build a
future,
Love is great until they see it takes more than love to build on,
We will need to put up a fight until our wants and needs become
LOVE.

You were all I needed until my heart was left cold.

Tainted Love

Finding that one person is all we want,
We can remember that special day our feelings were all over the
place,
That first kiss, those details pushed us to the limit while falling
deeper in LOVE.
But that one thing that made you regret giving your heart away,
Pushed you into a place that made you give up on LOVE and
LIFE.

When I told you there was nobody like me, I meant just that.

No Love Lost

After everything has taken place, you can smile again.
It took you some time to accept that things were not going to
work out.
All the text messages are erased; now, it's time to open your
heart up again.
The day you choose to give someone your heart is the day they
come back knocking on yours.

Just a Thought

Take every experience as a lesson,
Within that broken place, you will find the strength,
Make sure you give yourself time to heal from a broken heart,
So you are not cutting others while LOVING them.

HEALING

If loving you is wrong, if I gave you my heart, is it even worth the fight.

Looking for peace is what we really want--finding a place to rest our hearts while allowing this pain to suffocate our thoughts.

I killed a part of myself LOVING you.

You will never understand the damage until someone tries to
LOVE you.

Let me Go

You came back just to see if I was still hurting,
I thought you had someone else,
Knowing I was not worth the fight,
We pushed each other to the limit.
Allowing our hearts to suffocate from the past,
If you wanted me,
If what we had really mattered,
You 'wouldn't be concerned with what others thought.

Hearing the song we both LOVED allowed me to understand
how much it really hurt.

Turning the Page

Moving past this place is never easy,
Allowing someone in after walking away will take time,
Jumping into another relationship will not bring healing,
But getting over them, One day at a time.

Everything reminds me of you, I've tried killing the part of me that still loves you.

The Process

If we could forget about it?
If only erasing memories were as simple as clearing a hard drive
Real Love doesn't die because you want it to.
We get used to dealing with the pain until we accept things are
over.

LOVING you has changed my life forever.

An Open Book

I was scared to love;
Opening myself exposed my scars.
But you accepted me when no one could see past my pain.
Taking your time, I was able to trust again, but talking allowed
me to move past the pain.
And I want to say,
Thank you.

You never noticed me because while my eyes were focused on
you, your eyes were looking everywhere else

A Closed Heart

We gave our hearts away too soon,
The way you LOVED me was misunderstood,
How can someone LOVE a heart that's broken?
She looked past my pain and saw my heart,
But my fear of letting her in pushed her away,
Until the day she walked out of my life.

I thought I was over you until I heard your voice.

Heartless

Nobody heard my cry; my words were always misunderstood,
Those late nights trying to find someone to listen to my
heartbeat,
Everyone said let me love you, and I will love away the pain.
But loving me took a special person that understood my heart
beats a certain way.

With every tear, a piece of me was dying as you walked away.

Letting Go

The hardest thing about Love them is letting go.
Those promises that were made are engraved in your heart,
They hold vital information and secrets that have created a bond
that has been broken,
Facing your fears will always leave you questioning who
you are.
One day at a time, it will get easier,
Through it all, make sure you are real with yourself,

Called, I didn't answer; it gave me peace knowing how strong I
really am.

Voicemail

Looking back, I never thought I could get over you until your
call went to voicemail,
You ignored me when I tried to work things out,
Our past was nothing but secrets revealed through the way we
dealt with this pain,
Begging for your Love was not working, so what was the reason
to keep fighting?
Knowing you still love me didn't allow you to see I was fighting
for your heart.
It was nothing more than a show for you while watching my
heart turn cold.

They want you because they cannot have you

Reflection of my Heart

I used to ask myself, is the journey the same as falling in love?
How can two hearts collide, but when it's over one is left
suffocating?
Trying to reverse these feelings was not easy, as you took a piece
of my heart with you,
That same day I looked in the mirror, not longing for someone
else to love me,
But for me to start Loving myself.

'LOVE'S first commandment:
Forgive those who have hurt you

Past the pain

Moving past this place was never easy,
Knowing we created a bond that no longer holds any value,
If I was ever going to heal, I had to forgive myself, including
you,
Holding you hostage in my heart would never solve anything,
But letting you go to be loved again gave us both the healing we
needed.

After Everything was done, I wanted to keep pressing the issue;
how did we get to this place

Closed Door

Today, you will need to decide if loving them is killing you.
Every breath has caused you to look at things differently,
The reality of love is death; one day it will end,
But true love will live forever after two souls have said goodbye.

Yesterday, I deleted your pictures and erased your voicemails.
Everything that reminded me of you is gone.
Except for the stains you left on my heart

In My Feelings

Every day, you look for a reason to keep living,
A broken heart will leave you feeling hopeless in a world that
paints an image,
That you fight for what you want until the end.
But in the end, chasing someone to love you is never the answer,
If they cannot love you for who you are, then, it's not love.

Waking up to an empty bed, rolling over, looking at pictures of you still sitting on my nightstand. I used to cry, now all I do is smile

One Day at a Time

Do you know how long I've waited for this day?
Now, whenever you cross my mind, I don't get stressed out.
It took some time, but with every day that goes by, I find a piece
of my heart that's regenerating.

Just a Thought

Face the facts, look at where you are, nothing you say or do will change what has taken place. You were built for this very moment.

THIS HEART

Your heart is the entrance to your soul,
thinking it would last for eternity,
While loving you has given me new life

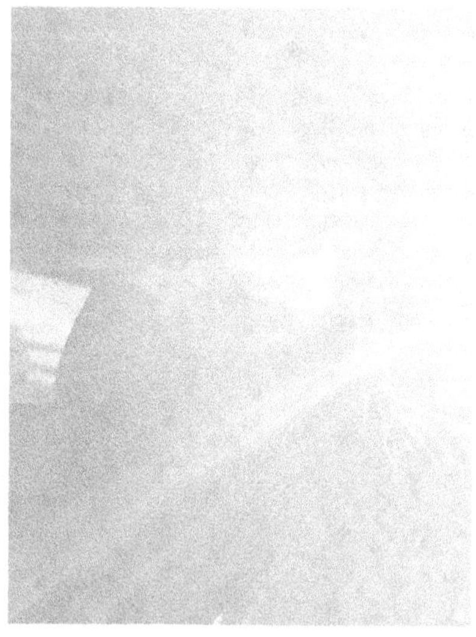

After the pain has subsided, 'you're ready to open up again

Just when you feel like the test is over,
You have gotten to a place of healing,
Is when love knocks on your heart, asking if you are ready.

"You never noticed me because while my eyes were focused on
you, your eyes were looking everywhere else."

Him: You don't say much anymore.
Her: *Drowning in her own mind, words are never enough.*
Him: I gave you my heart.
Her: You never gave me your time.

I miss the person I thought you were

Love at First Sight
We met on a full moon,
Time stood still while I looked into your eyes,
Your hair was perfect, flowing with the breeze,
Our conversation created an instant bond.
Everything about you was what I needed,
My dreams became a reality,
Because you were my LOVE.

Don't awaken love until it's the proper time.

53

The Echoes

I thought you would see a difference,
But you went on like nothing happened,
Everyone told me how good I looked,
I still felt lonely,
Because it didn't come from you.

"I've broken a million hearts trying to find true love."

Bleeding on You

Was it love I really wanted?
Or someone to fill a void?
From Those who slipped through my hands,
Left me clinching on love support,
If they couldn't give me what I needed,
I would find it somewhere else,
From heart to heart,
Not realizing love doesn't live here anymore.

"It took years to find myself, and when I did, my heart was cold."

What is Left

Truth is, I still loved her,
Even after the heartbreak,
You walking out of my life.
Trying to find the courage,
Was it ever enough?
Giving my all,
To someone who no longer looked at me the same,
They still expect responsiveness,
Without touch.
What was I holding on to?
Was it the memories,
Or the fact of losing someone,
That no longer loves me?

"I would spill my soul with words that feel on shallow hearts."

His Heart

I was told:
I'm too sensitive,
Maybe her idea of love was misunderstood,
Loving her was more of a challenge,
Flowers and foot rubs were no longer appreciated
Expressing my feelings was never enough,
The more I did, the door was slowly closing,
Until the day you gave up on us....

"She loved me until she realized that loving me wasn't enough."

Let Me In

Let me peel away the layers,
That has been formed from the pain,
The brokenness and promises that have left you
Feeling cold at night.
Many came only to use your body,
Claiming they love you.
Every time being let down, not believing if real love will
Ever exist.

"I thought me changing would reunite our love, only to realize
your heart was somewhere else."

Writing on the Wall

I was still in love with her,
After the letdowns,
Her arrogance pushes her to ignore what's real,
She walks around like Everything is great.
Nobody wants to talk about what is going on.
How much longer can I hold on?
When it's all said and done, you will see, I was worth it

"The greatest feeling is being in love with someone that loves you back."

My Heart

I just want to be held.
I just want to be loved.
I just want to be heard.
I need to know, do you still care?

"After everything, they will see you were worth the fight, but
it'll be too late."

One Day

The same person that ignored you.
The one who didn't see your worth.
That dragged your name through the mud.
Only to see they gave up because of what everyone else thought.
After your heart has healed,
And feelings are a distant memory,
The goal is to walk away keeping secrets.

"I loved who you were when you didn't even see your worth."

Broken

I've wrapped my heart around you,
But realized it wasn't enough,
Broken from what has taken place,
My touch left cuts,
Unheard words became fears,
Echoes turned into memories,
We walked away confused,
Not able to talk,
With nothing left.

Just a Thought

Keep his attention, or someone else will. Give her the LOVE she needs, or what you have will die slowly.

Distant Lovers

To love again,
To have someone to be loved,
Do you know who I am?
Can I share my goals with you?
Fighting for attention,
Only to feel alone,
In a sexless relationship,
Trying to hold on.
When you ignore where we are at,
I looked into your eyes,
My reflection was not there,
I touched your soul,
To see if the key would fit.
Looking for answers,
Thinking it was a dream,
Only to realize,
You didn't love me anymore.

"My greatest fear was losing you only to realize I lost myself trying to love you."

What If

I fell in love just for you to walk away.
Listening to the door close,
Left a hole in me.
But I still believed in us.
Every hour I prayed that you would return.
Our hearts torn apart from words.
Text messages to voicemails,
We ignored our feelings only to question,
Our LOVE

"You gave me your heart, I gave you a promise until the end of time."

The Void

I had it all but no longer had you.
Thinking opening my heart up would heal those wounds,
They came in, rearranging my heart,
Pictures of you were still in place.
They asked questions,
To see I was still in LOVE with you,
I wanted someone to fill this void,
To take away this pain,
But this heart was still yours.

"Falling in love is not a choice; it just happens."

My Queen

She saw more in me than I could understand,
She challenged me to change,
Her touch calmed the storms in me,
She didn't complain.
She spoke life,
Her words opened my heart,
Everything about her,
Allowed me to grow.
This woman gave me new life,
To LOVE again,
When I didn't trust,
After I let myself down,
That was the day,
I was ready to love again.

"I almost gave up on you until I saw how much you really loved me."

Just a Thought

Her LOVE is more than what you can consume. She opened his eyes to a world that gave him hope. Because of you, I can love can again. I still long for you…Even when I cannot feel your touch.

"How do you love someone in the dark? By listening to the beat
of their heart."

These Walls

If these walls could speak, what would be said?
Echoes from our hearts,
From the pain that tore us apart,
How can we rebuild this love?
If we never make time,
If we never listen to those heartbeats,
We will never know,
How to love again.

"We met when our hearts were still tangled from the past."

Let Me In

It was late at night,
Didn't expect the conversation to draw us in,
Her heartbeat was different,
It was as gentle as her voice.
Listening to her explain her past,
She looked in the mirror,
I saw the light in her eyes,
But the pain from our past,
Allowed us to open up,
Because we both bleed from the same place.
Her words gave me hope,
My words gave her understanding,
But the both of us were still hurting,
Not from wanting LOVE,
But making the same mistake.

"If you give me your heart, I promise I will not hurt it."

Your Heart

The hardest part about love,
Is giving someone power to hurt you,
Being vulnerable while looking over your shoulder,
Allowing them to make your heart their home.
Can I trust you?
What do you really want?
Will you be like everyone else
That came and left?
Hoping you understand,
I gave it all up to just love you.

"I've got to be honest, I entertained some great women but
wasn't ready."

Honest

They had it all together,
I was still hurt from my ex,
Everything a man could dream of,
Every day I would open up.
Then closed like a clam,
My heart was cold,
Even the LOVE they gave wasn't enough,
When I walked away,
They didn't understand.
Yes, I was a good man,
But a MAN that wasn't ready.

"A man will never be faithful until he finds himself."

His Reflection

He looked in the mirror,
And realized life had no meaning,
Unless he was able to share it with someone,
So, he looked for LOVE.
Searching in the sheets,
It wasn't enough,
Everyone that crossed his path,
Would slip through his fingers.
Years of breaking hearts,
That's when he broke his OWN,
From the woman he truly LOVED,
Thinking that she would return.
He promised never to LOVE again,
Until his heart was ready.

"Nobody understood what I was looking for until I found you."

I'm Still Waiting

She was everything I prayed for,
Every night I woke up just to stare at her,
Lost in between my dreams and reality,
It still wasn't enough.
We thought LOVE would get us through,
Everyday it was something different,
Our backs met late at night,
Words became text messages.
Touching you brought chills up your spin,
The LOVE we shared,
Was a distant memory?

"You will never be enough to someone that doesn't understand how to LOVE you."

Questions

Why do you LOVE ME?
Was one of the questions I would often ask.
Not expecting them to understand.
But hopefully, they would see my worth.
They would raise the standard to what we both needed.
Taking your time to learn my every move.
Understanding that my past placed up high walls.
And my present pushes my thoughts with questions.

"I've lost trust in LOVE only to make excuses."

Until the End

They promise you: until death do us part,
The power to love is to give your heart away,
But real LOVE is always tested,
When everyone else gave up.
I held on just to watch you walk away,
My trust was broken,
While watching my world crumble,
Those who endure until the end,
Ran out of excuses.

"Loving you has changed me."

This Love

Just when you think it couldn't happen,
Is when they touch your soul,
The power to LOVE is never by choice,
It's a gift that many never prepare for.
Many came and left,
Not knowing we would be without them,
The intent of falling in love is never easy,
Even after you have given someone else power to hurt you,
Her love changed me…
I was able to understand,
That I had to endure the pain from my past,
And then I realized I wasn't ready until my wounds were
completely healed.
When She came, it was least expected it,
Late-night conversations,
Early morning texts,
Her love changed me…
Her love comforted me…
Her LOVE gave me new life.

"If I gave you time, would you give me your heart?"

Ready for Love

Phone calls turned into meeting up,
There wasn't a day we didn't hear from each other,
Everything evolved around us,
Our goals and what we wanted.
Time was spent listening and learning,
That our hearts were ready,
But moving past what has taken place,
Was never easy.
We embraced that opening the door too soon,
Will bring up old wounds,
If we crossed the line,
Would it make us ready?
Or would it make us regret,
That Love is more than just a feeling?
It is time that we can never get back.

"Letting you in wasn't easy after so many failed relationships."

Never Give Up

No matter what,
It was not easy giving you my heart,
The power to heal or tear me apart,
Lost in-between, should I prepare myself for
Her walking away,
Will she LOVE who I truly am?
Or see what my past LOVE couldn't accept?
This MAN has fallen in LOVE
Just To run away from it.
It wasn't that she couldn't fulfill my needs,
A heart never forgets those experiences,
When he tried to fight for Love,
When he gave his heart away,
It wasn't enough,
Even for the right woman.

"I gave up when you walked away."

Misunderstood

How long will this heart bleed?
On love support,
Everyone claims to have the cure,
Let me LOVE you,
I'm nothing like her.
He was Loving with an open wound,
Deep cuts from the past,
Bleeding on those who crossed my heart,
Nothing He did could bury this pain.
Those who came and left could only,
Give me temporary satisfaction,
She understood that nothing could make me love her more,
Until He was ready.

"Love is more than just a thought, but placed into the wrong
hands, it can destroy the strongest person."

Ready for LOVE

He moved on,
With the intent to never love again,
It wasn't that he did want to,
He refused to give someone the power
To destroy his heart.
Every year, he would relive those mistakes,
The broken promises,
Hearts scattered from memories,
Until he was bold enough to let go.
Ready for whatever came his way,
Those who left might have left footprints,
But didn't leave him heartless.

"She told me I deserve someone that will see the best in me, who will trust and love me blindly, I told her I'm ready."

Ready to Love

Who prepares themselves to LOVE?
Is it that state of loneliness that pushes us to explore?
Or is it us missing those who walked away?
With pieces of our HEART,
If I waited for those who left,
I would hold everyone accountable for not LOVING me
correctly.
Giving you myself required
letting down my walls,
With both of us wanting the same thing, it was easier,
To Love again,
To breathe.
Left us taking a late-night walk on the beach,
Holding you made my world feel complete,
Just when I said it wasn't possible,
You came into my life,
Making it complete.

"She gave me a reason to Love again."

This LOVE

Words could never describe this feeling,
There were days it was hard to function,
My thoughts were in the clouds,
She accepted who I was,
And understood my past.
Her LOVE made me a better man,
Our conversations allowed me to understand,
Why I fell in LOVE so fast,
It was more than just a feeling.
A lifetime of getting answers from past situations,
I was able to accept or feel like,
My past was a complete failure,
Or was it me learning how to LOVE myself?

"I need you more than my next breath."

She Calmed the Beast in Me

Words were more than thoughts.
I used to think
There was no place in my HEART for you,
I wasn't worthy of your embrace,
All the reasons for not having someone,
Allowed me to let go of my past.
We met on a full moon,
And That very night,
The chains were released from around my HEART,
Her words captivated my soul.
On that night, I was free,
Now I get to express myself without being judged,
From my temptations, dreams, fears,
I can be myself,
And she will still LOVE who I am.

"The greatest feeling is when they can LOVE you even when
things are not right."

Her Love

Our fights would push me into a corner,
I didn't know how to adjust,
So, ignoring issues like they never existed was how I dealt with
confrontation.
Not knowing how to communicate put a wedge between us,
She didn't stop touching my heart,
Her words were soft and southing,
And that is when I began to open up more.
Even when things were wrong,
She never stopped taking care of my needs,
The consistency this woman had,
Made me deal with issues head-on.

"Can I trust you enough to share my deepest secrets?"

Book of Love

We shared secrets,
No pages were left unturned,
It was an open book,
Time created a bond,
Days and nights left us feeling complete,
But it was more than what we expected,
Even with what was presented,
Taking our time writing on each other's hearts,
With what we feared the most,
The pages of our life become an open book of love.

"One day, you will understand why it didn't work out."

Torn Pages

She looked at me with tears running down her face,
You deserve someone who can see your worth,
Doing everything in my power to make her stay,
She left without giving me a reason,
My thoughts were all over the place,
Maybe I wasn't good enough?
Maybe she found someone who could give her the world?
Then I realized,
Her walking away made me a better man,
Even after the breakup,
I still played my hand,
Trying to win her back only to see,
Her heart was somewhere else,
The PAIN brought out the best in me,
Every day a page of my life was ripped away,
Promises were smeared on torn pages left behind.

"I used to be scared of death; now, I am scared of LOVE."

Ready or Not

He wanted to let her in but was afraid,
Those who came and left,
Still had a hold on his emotions,
Even after GOD placed a gem in his life,
He still questioned if he was worthy of it.
After being broken-hearted,
He looked at every woman the same way,
What do you want with a man like me?
Past lovers came just to use me up,
Then left without a trace,
So what made her any different?
Love couldn't exist until he was ready,
Opening up and accepting that being scared of LOVE,
Made him only give half.

"Life without you is like death times two."

Let's Be Honest

Looking back on how it all happened,
Made me appreciate her for sticking around as long as she did,
Even after the lies and betrayal that took place,
She just wanted me and the truth from my lips.
Her LOVE was deeper than what this heart could embrace,
She cried a thousand times in my arms,
Thinking that Holding her would make things right,
With every touch her body trembled.
Her face placed on my chest,
Felt like home,
watching her cry from my own selfishness,
Opened up Pandora's Box.
Trying everything in my power to lift her spirits,
That very day, our hearts were torn into two.

"I failed a thousand times just to find you."

From Boys to Men

Many gave up when I kept on searching,
It challenged every part of my life,
No longer was it about me,
But finding the right one that's a part of my destiny.
In the past, all I wanted was LOVE,
But finding someone who was consistent wasn't easy,
So, I went from looking to praying,
From praying to waiting,
From waiting until the time was right.
I used to rush what I wanted,
Now I'm allowing time to have her perfect work,
When we found each other, it wasn't the perfect situation,
But the wait taught me how to make the right choices,
And not to make the same mistakes.

"This thing called LOVE will turn on you without any notice.
Don't lose hope because they want to walk away."

Moment of Truth

She knew my every move,
When I was hungry, when I needed to be left alone.
But she couldn't understand the sudden change,
There were days her distance made me wonder,
What was I doing wrong?
I thought she stuck around because of LOVE,
It was really about her getting the courage to move on.
One day, she woke up, and that's when she said,
"I want a divorce because I'm not happy."
My heart stopped.
Nothing I said would change her mind,
She was content with her decision,
I didn't know how to react,
Trying to ease the pain,
Pushed me to that place,
When all I did was ask questions,
Do you Love me?
Is there someone else?
And that's when she said, "I do love you, but I'm not in Love
with you."

"That moment of loneliness will always push you into the wrong arms."

Let Me Love You

Everyone who crossed my path always wanted a history report,
The pain was still fresh,
Trying to ease the pain by drowning my heart in her arms,
Left a bitter taste in my mouth,
I was ready to fall in LOVE,
But was I ready for commitment?
Anyone who gave me attention had me wrapped,
Those who came were everything a man could want,
Conversations turned into feelings,
And feelings turned into us expressing our LOVE,
But catching my heart wasn't easy.
While facing my fears and my feelings,
It all came out,
Thought I was over her,
That is when I realized, she still had a piece of my heart.

"If I had one last wish, let this love outlast any situation."

One Day at a Time

She couldn't understand why I always smiled,
Through the ups and downs,
The broken promises that couldn't get fixed,
I stood strong with that same smile,
Believing that our love could last a lifetime,
Nothing was different,
We fussed and fought all night,
Falling asleep with our backs turned,
Pushed us further away from dealing with our pain.
She made me stronger,
What we dealt showed us,
That love is more than just emotions,
It's two hearts fighting for attention,
Two souls wanting to be touched,
But will we hear the answers?

"I found myself before finding love in a lonely place."

Missed Text Messages

It was worth the wait,
Those who came couldn't understand,
But you'll know when it's the right time,
Refusing to make the same mistakes of me being lonely,
Every day I worked on me finding out who I am.
Some days I wanted to send a text,
Saying, *"Wyd? I am thinking about you,"*
But that place of loneliness will push you,
Into loving someone out of want,
Until my heart pushed me to that place,
And my thoughts allowed me to see,
I never forgave myself.

"She looked at me and said, I could be better for you."

She Added Value

The existence of what we want,
Versus what we need can be confusing,
Nobody wants to continue giving their heart away,
To never trust again.
It took a while for me to open up,
This woman pushed me and made me understand,
Until you can be real with yourself, nothing will go right.
My thoughts, *It's impossible to love me correctly,*
She found out everything about me,
Because she didn't want to hurt me,
She found out why I was so closed.
What took place that made me so reserved,
Her touch made me see,
That love is still real,
Once your scars have healed,
You will see how she makes you better.

"Understanding that what was needed in my life was her."

An Open Book

Every day would start off with me being thankful,
For what was presented and what was ahead,
Being a man that was taught how to pray,
Made it easier to deal with certain situations.
Every woman that came taught me something,
What to expect and what not to accept,
Then it happened,
On a cold night, she touched my heart,
Our conversation awakened my desires,
It was like old times staying on the phone all night,
Her patience showed me she was serious.
Taking my time building a bond with her,
Allowed me to move past,
Those who broke my heart,
Allowed me to become an open book.

"One day, you will see why they couldn't be a part of your future."

Wanted Time

I tried to make her stay,
Nothing I did would convince her to see how much I loved her,
I looked for answers only to get the same results,
Text messages were ignored,
Sending gifts through the mail, no response,
Flowers left on the steps were left outside,
Was I dumb for trying to win back the woman I love?
Or fighting a battle that was already over?
Maybe she wasn't the type to fight,
Or she didn't understand that you fight to stay in LOVE,
Every day I would look for a reason to talk to her,
Only to see her heart was somewhere else.
Even after planning my future with her,
I had to accept that a future with her didn't exist,
Because, to her, my time her didn't matter.

"Until we face our own demons, everything we touch will slip
through our grip."

Ready or Not

My heart was open,
To everyone that pursued me,
It wasn't about playing the hand that was dealt,
I wanted to weigh my options and not rush.
Falling into the same trap again,
My heart might have been ready, but the pain was still fresh,
Thinking that if I gave someone my time,
It would help with moving past the struggles.
After being with someone that didn't understand who I was,
Made it hard to accept compliments from others,
What they saw in me,
The one I still had feelings for never acknowledged.
So, a desperate heart was on the loose,
From heart to heart he went,
Until he found the one that understood his pain,
She was open and ready with a past that
Exposed his mask.
She understood why he couldn't settle,
She knew that falling in love would not make things better,
He tried to keep her around,
And that's when she said, "You're not ready for LOVE."

"Some things will take years to get over, but never close your heart to the possibilities of falling in LOVE again."

Let's Be Honest

A closed heart will never understand,
Never force what you are not ready for,
Finding the strength to move on is never easy,
But accepting the challenge is what makes us stronger.
Those who came and left taught us a lesson,
The sad thing is,
We only remember the pain due to where we are at,
And that's when you need to be honest.
Are you ready for LOVE?
Or should you take out time to deal with your scars?
If we are not honest with what we want,
We will never move past what has taken place,
And that's the reason most relationships never evolve,
Because the idea of love is,
Being with someone that loves you, but,
How can you receive what you are not ready for?
Why give someone your heart when your heart is somewhere
else?
Let's be honest, your heart is still closed,
Until you deal with the pain,
Your heart will only be a temporary resting place.

I thought about going back, then I remembered you really didn't love me like you said."

What If

After the break-up,
I tried finding you in everyone else,
And that's when I looked in the mirror,
Understood that loving you didn't change my life,
You leaving me did;
Even with the way things ended,
Our hearts were still entangled,
We never crossed the line.
But I thought about the possibilities of us reuniting,
What would change?
Can we start all over and make it right?
Or are we fighting a battle that's already over?

"After a long day of trying to find peace, she was my therapy."

Be My Peace

I didn't have to tell her how I was feeling,
She would look into my eyes,
And understand all I needed to do was rest,
Her words were few because talking would frustrate me.
She had all the answers but still let me lead the way,
Her voice brought peace when I was upset,
Many asked how I found a woman like her,
Knowing I could have been with anyone.
I never second-guessed my decision,
My life was a lot better knowing we could talk things out,
When things weren't right,
Even if it took days,
She would find a way to reason,
Everything about her made my life better,
Because she was my Peace.

"I gave it all up just to have you, not looking back on what could have been."

Can I Trust You

I used to live for the moment,
Thinking I was missing out on something,
Never giving my all because,
Trusting someone was not easy,
Truth be told, they might have you and still be entertaining
others,
But it's not fair holding someone accountable for a past lover's
actions.
It was hard letting them in,
But it was always easy letting them walk away,
How could I continue to do this and expect anyone to commit?
Everyone that came said, 'Let me in,
I can love you,
I'm nothing like her.'
After finding out about my past,
It made it easy for them to love the man I am,
They saw past my flaws and saw my worth,
And that was the day my heart opened.

"When you find the magic in someone, it will change your life forever."

Soul Searching

Nothing surprises me anymore,
But finding someone who can spark a flame,
Within your soul is rare,
When you're used to dealing with people who think
It's all about them,
Then you find someone that puts your needs ahead of theirs.
They are always thinking of ways to make,
The relationship healthier,
We all have dealt with those who used us,
Then tried to make us feel bad because we refused to
be used by them.
Life is short, and love doesn't always come around.

"Broken hearts will always remember those who did them
wrong."

Breakup to Makeup

After the break-up,
Our lives took on a new meaning,
Secrets that were exchanged become an open book,
Those who we thought were on our side,
Found a reason to stir up what went down,
We just wanted to be happy,
It didn't mean everyone else had to understand,
But we had a good handle on our approach,
The feelings were still strong,
But not strong enough to keep us together,
She wanted more out of me,
I wanted more out of her,
But the more we gave, the more we drew apart,
Fighting for attention only to see,
We just couldn't get it right,
And when we did,
It was too late.

"Many walked away realizing they should never have left."

Until the End of Time

The grass always looks greener from a distance,
But the closer you get, you will see the same weeds,
I used to admire other couples who had the perfect relationship,
And that's when I found out they have the same issues we dealt
with.
There weren't any secrets,
They just didn't give up,
The fight for love was about,
Not allowing others to influence what they had.
The outlet wasn't posting their problems,
They dealt with it behind closed doors,
Praying with each other,
And never letting the opinions of others dictate what they had.
Communication was the key,
As they strived for perfection,
Many couples looked at them saying,
"I am surprised you all are still together."
After many walked away,
Now regret their decision,
They understood that real love,
Fights until the end.

"Those who are jealous of what you have will always find a reason to speak down on your relationship."

Jezebel

We all have made plenty of mistakes trying to get it right,
While everyone was trying to find a reason to leave,
I was praying she would find a reason to stay,
But everyone knew what was best for her.
Holding onto secrets while we walked away empty,
Hiding our feelings because of what everyone thought,
Many said I hope you work it out,
But they hated that we still had a close bond.
We didn't understand the effect others had on our decision,
Until you saw it yourself,
Those who stood with you,
Where the same people that had so much control in your life.
As time went on, you played the game,
Looking for my attention only to see I wasn't a part of it
anymore,
My time was well spent not letting others run my life,
Only to see you still allowed them to run yours.

"Don't allow distraction to stop you from seeing the signs."

Listen to Your Heart

We fell in love,
Even when things weren't right,
Trying to keep what we had sacred wasn't easy,
But we made it work.
She always found something wrong with me,
I wasn't her type;
Her past involved men who were disrespectful,
Even after my affection, it wasn't enough.
Trying to prove my love to her,
Made me check myself,
Was I giving her what she needed?
Or was I selling myself short?
Thinking if I walked away now it would be easier,
But my heart wouldn't allow me to,
Late nights turned into us sitting across from each other,
Conversations were cut short,
We stayed because we longed for love,
Only to end up ignoring the signs.

"Changing who you are will not allow them to love you any differently."

Me, Myself, and I

Thinking that if I fit what she wanted,
It would make her want me more,
Looking into her past,
She never had anyone like me.
Even with me being so caring,
It wasn't enough to keep her happy,
Was it me, or maybe she didn't appreciate who I was?
Time went on, and we got even closer,
I found myself doing things just to make her happy,
Breaking out of my box,
Put a smile on her face,
Thinking to myself,
It's not that bad.
Anything to keep a smile on her face,
But that wasn't enough,
Because I was still the same man,
I had to keep it real with myself and everyone else around me.
Then I understood,
I was changing just to please her,
And it still didn't make her stay.

"I was ready for you, but were you ready for me?"

Circle of Love

Sometimes, things come back around full circle,
We both weren't happy and were looking for more,
In passing, we knew each other,
My life was different than yours.
On a day I least expected,
You walked past me and caught my attention,
The attraction was already there,
All it took was conversation and chemistry.
Us hitting it off on the first date,
Not knowing if it was what we wanted,
Time made everything perfect as our love grew,
Our promise was to make it last forever.
So, us cutting everyone off,
Made us want more than just a physical relationship,
As time went on,
You questioned if we should go any further,
Because fighting for love shouldn't be this exhausting,
Only to see you weren't ready.

"Our approach is always based on our last situation."

Her

Knowing I was ready to move forward,
It was about me taking my time,
Those who came where looking for something long term,
I was honest and wanted to take my time.
With every encounter, I always compared it to *her*,
Nobody wants to get caught up,
Just have someone else walk out of their life,
So, my approach had to be different.
Being I love hard, and put my all on the line,
I couldn't give my heart away too soon,
Until I met *her*,
She was open and understood why I couldn't open up too fast.
We both came out of similar situations,
And it made it interesting to see where we would end up,
Our hearts were ready for love,
But our walls were still up.
Every day, opening up became easy,
Late night talks pushed us to revealing our darkest secrets,
I've learned until we can talk about the things we struggle with,
Every relationship will never evolve.

"An open heart will always be ready to learn something new."

My Teacher

Knowing my past was not squeaky clean,
I was open to answering questions about it,
With nothing to hide, my life was an open book,
Even with me being honest, many couldn't handle the truth.
I wasn't trying to run anyone off,
They just needed to know what I've dealt with,
Many came expecting more,
But I took my time letting anyone in.
Then my heart was open,
We both spoke the same language,
But even with that,
It was about teaching each other how to love.
What we both experienced taught us a lot,
And vowed never to relive it,
The challenges we faced taught us,
It's ok to listen,
Because listening will teach you how to love.

I looked at her and said, "All I want is you."

You

From a distance, she caught my eye,
Everything about her was different,
We met on the hottest day of the year,
Never thought it would be love at first sight.
Her mind was on another level,
Talking about politics to money matters,
Break was over, so she had to leave,
Watching her walk from a distance,
Her hair was flowing with the wind,
The scent she left behind,
Lingered in the room for a minute.
I had to have her in my life,
Until she became my wife,
It was Everything I dreamed of,
She gave me a reason to believe in love again,
Until she said, 'We are better off as friends".

No Love Lost

They would only call when they needed something,
You really didn't exist,
It was all about them and what they could get from you,
Those text messages got ignored.
You were just like anyone else in their contacts,
Then there was a day you gave up,
On trying to show you care,
Proving you still want to work through the issues.
Each day got a little bit easier,
A month later, you were almost there,
Because they weren't getting your attention,
Then your phone went off.

WYD?

When you wanted a response,
They never responded.
Now time has gone by,
You have moved on,
They want to see where your heart is,
And now, you want my love?

"I used to think something was wrong with me only to see it was you."

Mirror on the Wall

What was wrong with me?
Was I too much or not enough?
We took on two different paths,
Then we couldn't make our minds up,
If we wanted each other or ignored what we have,
After trying to fix the problem,
Nothing made us happy.
We found peace with others,
Life pushed us to distance ourselves,
But always had something negative to say,
Nothing I did made you see,
All I wanted was you.
Time went, and you found fault in Everything I did,
It was never about the issues you had,
I was silent even when I wanted to explode,
Until fighting Love left us hopeless.

"You were my world; everything else was just a dream until I found you."

12/12/12

Love was created on this day,
We knew nothing would tear us apart,
Our lives took on a new meaning,
Knowing we could make this last forever.
I remember the look in your eyes,
Your heart was open,
Tears flooded my face,
With every step you took,
Made me see why I chose you.
It was the happiest day of my life,
Those we loved from near and far,
Came to celebrate that moment,
And the love we shared,
Changed our life forever.

"I have drowned every day just to be in your arms."

His Pain

My heart felt cold without you,
Every night was just a dream,
Of me missing you,
Waiting for your return.
Many came, but it was only temporary satisfaction,
I tried finding you in every one I was with,
Left me looking for love in the wrong places,
My broken heart was filled with poison.
Everyone I touched felt my pain,
They wanted in only to see my heart was closed,
It wasn't about what they could offer,
In their thoughts,
How could I help him move past his pain?
Until a man has healed,
He will hurt every woman he comes across.

"Let's not allow others to ruin what took us years to build."

Keeping Secrets

Everyone always knows what's best,
Family and friends will always get in the way,
When things are not right,
If we continue to let, them speak on what is best.
They will eventually have control,
After the fights, we tend to look for an outlet,
Looking for someone to vent to,
Pushing us into the wrong arms,
Opening up Pandora's box,
Just to bring family and friends,
Into our relationship,
It took years to get here,
It will take more to love you the right way,
Let's fight for love,
And what we believe in,
As we build on a dynasty of Love.

"What did you expect Love was, a fairy tale?"

Fairytale

We always wanted the perfect relationship,
But compared it to what we had seen in others,
Watching our parents and family's relationships,
We saw how to love,
And what to expect.
In our imperfections, there is a lesson,
It will never be about the night in shining armor,
But a man that can be stable,
It's *never* about the woman that can handle a million tasks,
But a woman that is balanced.
We tend to fight against our dreams,
For what is reality,
But never sell yourself short,
Just to have temporary love.

"You will learn that Love will cost you everything, including
your life."

The Perfect Match

My heart was set on making things better,
She gave me her all,
I promised to give my life,
We both came out of very similar situations.
Our past mirrored,
And we didn't want to relive it,
Just like any other couple, work kept us busy,
But making time was very tricky.
So, thinking outside of the box was what I loved,
No matter what we did for each other,
Even with us being so open,
We still looked for something to happen.
The past had us so shaken,
Things were too perfect to be true,
We didn't keep secrets,
Our life was an open book.
No hiding our feelings until we got upset,
It was Everything we both wanted,
And promised never to hold back.

"Make sure your heart is pure before giving it away."

313

Heart On a Platter

My past was filled with letdowns,
Giving my all just to fail,
But learning from my mistakes made me want more,
Those who left didn't understand how to fight,
It was really all about them,
Until they realize,
You will fight in every relationship.
When I wanted to give my heart away,
I withheld my feelings due to my past,
So, she presented hers,
Allowing me to see she was serious,
Even with my heart being ready,
I still had reservations,
If I trust you with my heart,
Will you still walk away?
Should I give you the power to hurt me,
With this thing called Love?

"You might be ready to love, but are you ready for the pain too?"

Love and Pain

Thinking I know who she is,
Based on our time together,
Is never enough,
You will never know someone until you make them upset,
After the love has faded off,
And reality has set in,
You will see that love is more about compromise,
But who is willing to do that?
We have given our all just to come up short,
Feeling like what we do is never enough,
Just to end the call saying *I love you*,
Only to still feel a void,
Like what you give is overlooked,
And that is when you understand,
That with love comes pain,
It allows us to appreciate each other,
While learning how to Love.

"Moving forward requires us to stop looking back."

Please Forgive Me

Just when I was ok with my situation,
Is when things came back up,
Getting to a place of healing takes time,
Even when you have your thoughts together,
Be prepared for someone who will never let go
It's like they want to hold you hostage,
You accepted things did not last because of you,
But it's not good enough for them,
They want you to feel their pain for the rest of your life,
Maybe they haven't forgiven themselves,
Or maybe they haven't forgiven you.

"What are you willing to sacrifice for Love?"

Who Am I

If I gave it all up,
Would it be enough,
Convincing you that nothing else matters,
Sacrificing my time,
Giving you every second to keep you happy,
My life has no meaning without you,
Losing who I am just to keep you.
Is it worth the fight?
Is it worth the wait?
Or will I give it all just to lose you?

"She looked at him and said, I deserve more."

No More Pain

Her tears became a fortress,
Every night trying to erase what took place,
She gave her all,
Just to come up short,
If this was his idea of Love,
She didn't want any part of it,
The lies were more than her heart could take,
Looking for reasons to stay,
Gave her every reason to leave,
She was still in love,
But not in love with him.

"Her love wasn't enough for him to work things out."

The Exit

She was my dream that I held onto tight,
Never thought we would end up like this,
Our hearts were matched perfectly,
We could finish each other's sentences.
And that made us smile,
The connection was deeper than our understanding,
Until the usual happened,
Hearts were torn,
I was tired of waiting,
Longing for your love required me to sacrifice,
Playing the blame game,
And allowing everyone else's opinion to keep you complacent,
You didn't know what you wanted,
Years of fighting for your attention,
Only to see you were blind,
And putting others before me.
I had to accept the fact,
We, me, us…wasn't important,
It was all about,
What can I get from him?
If this was your way of showing Love,
I want no parts in it.

"Just when I thought I had you, is when I lost you."

What Do You Want

Torn between waiting or walking away,
It pushed me to a place of finding myself,
How do I heal while still loving you?
Nothing I said made you see,
We could work through this,
I would question, *where was her heart?*
Did I lose her before knowing it?
Or was her heart somewhere else?
There were days your distance was not from
Us being apart,
But you finding happiness away from me
Left you feeling whole.
Fighting for you to see it can work,
Even with a different approach,
I lost you even when I had you.

"The pain made us better."

We Made It

How we make it,
Just when we felt like giving up,
Is when we found the strength,
People couldn't understand that your heart was still broken,
While everyone else was jumping from relationships,
You were preparing yourself to love again,
But even when we thought we were ready,
It made us second guess,
What kind of person we wanted,
The pain made us appreciate life,
And life pushed us to a place to love again.